Scorpio Season

Scorpio Season

Poems by

Kalina Smith

Cover design by Shay Culligan
Cover image by Shayna Bepple on Unsplash
Author photo by Kalina Smith

ISBN: 978-1-63980-803-8

Kelsay Books
502 South 1040 East, A-119
American Fork, Utah 84003
Kelsaybooks.com

Acknowledgements

I would like to acknowledge the journals who published work in this collection before I organized it.

The Cackling Kettle: "Orion's Killer"

Dipity: "Aubade with a Mockingbird Witness"

Down in the Dirt: "The B-Grandkid," "Written Archaeology"

Ink & Marrow: "Affectionate Artillery"

One Art, a Journal of Poetry: "She Wanted Purple Jeans for Christmas"

Tulsa Review: "Blackwork"

Wayfarer: "Moths Are Not Butterflies"

Thank you for giving a fledgling writer a chance. I will forever be grateful.

I would like to acknowledge first and foremost my family. My mother is my first reader and has been since I was a child, writing stories on notebook paper. My dad and my brother are also readers (though that may be reluctantly!). Regardless, they have loved and supported me through everything in my life, and I can't thank them enough for that.

I also have a great group of friends who read everything I throw at them and give me the best feedback: Alyssa, Chandler, Hunter, and Paige, I love you all with everything in me. Thank you for loving me unconditionally and always being there for me.

I would not be the writer I am today without my professors at Arkansas Tech University, namely Dr. Deborah Wilson, Dr. Sarah Stein, Dr. Arwen Taylor, Dr. Tori Sharpe, Dr. Emily Hoffman, and Dr. Paola Gemme. Your guidance and teaching will stay with me forever. That also goes for my MFA professors, Dr. Jeanetta Calhoun Mish and Mary Meriam.

—Kalina Smith

Contents

Scorpio Season   11
A Night in My Parents' Yard   12
She Wanted Purple Jeans for Christmas   14
The B-Grandkid   15
To Alyssa: 16
$15 Palm Reading   18
Written Archaeology   19
Familiar   21
I Chased You Off Because I Get Attached Too Quickly   22
What Little Remains   23
Moths Are Not Butterflies   24
Empty Calories   25
From the Dewy Screen Door   26
G-Note   28
Deconstruction Surgery   30
From the Perspective of the Boy I Wanted to Marry   31
Boughs of Melancholy   33
Affectionate Artillery   34
Aubade with a Mockingbird Witness   35
Blackwork   37
Drunk Feelings; Sober Thoughts   38
11:11 Isn't an Angel Number   39
Ghosted   40
Orion's Killer   41
On the One That Wasn't the One   42
That Time I Stole the Sky   43

Scorpio Season

Auburn leaves crush under my feet
as I walk next to camellias
and a rushing river pounds in my ears.

I remember Novembers past as I pull
my jacket around my shoulders.
How I was due on December 21st,
but made my arrival on the second day
of the eleventh month.
I refused to be a Capricorn,
knowing I belonged under
the Scorpio sign.
Eagles fly, lizards hide, but scorpions
sit in waiting, intense as the desert sun.
These are the ones with whom I identify,
for their passion and loyalty,
how they never strike first,
but will sting if provoked.

Goldenrod leaves fall around my feet
as I walk next to azaleas
and a pleasant brook drums in my ears.
My stinger hides behind my jacket,
but stays poised.

A Night in My Parents' Yard

On a humid night, I buried myself in delta mud
while a whippoorwill sang an obnoxious tune,
nagging chirruping to rouse me.
As I emerged from the mud, I caught a whiff
of honeysuckle and blackberries. A fence of
thorns kept me at bay, like a hound dog
in a tiny, gated yard.
The ground squelched under my bare feet.
I ambled with only the lemony half-moon
and occasional lightning bug
to brighten my way.

Sometimes I go searching in the dead of night
and I don't know what for,
stumbling blindly, cutting the soles of my feet
on sharp rocks and oak leaves
the autumn wind did not blow away.
Hoots from Great Horned Owls warn us
and the stray cats and dogs my mama feeds
kibble and leftovers-because she can't stand
to see a living thing go hungry
of coyotes and the occasional black panther.
They're not native to the area,
but one night, on a drive with my daddy,
one jumped out in front of his groaning truck,
and we looked at each other like hikers
coming upon a cryptid.
Maybe Bigfoot lives in those woods, too.

Maybe I was looking for him,
or maybe I was looking for that panther.
Its eyes glowed amber like the full moon,
paralyzing me when I was just a child,
and my parents seemed so young.
Now that I'm older, so are they
and I fear for them to age.

I wrapped my arms around myself.
Was it a sudden summer wind
that chilled me, or the thought
of my graying parents?
While the squirrels slept, a choir of bullfrogs sang
to remind me I wasn't alone. The coyotes might have
been prowling, but little brown bats also flew above my head.
If not for these creatures, I'd have been by myself
in the blackness as I heard the gurgling faucet of a creek.
The water was seductive, so I went in knee-deep,
the muddiness grazing my denim. The bream
nibbling at my toes and algae slipping through them.
Farther and farther from home,
I should have wondered why
I left my map at the house
and brought no flashlight,
stepping into dirty water
with cuts on my feet, directionless.

Amid sycamore branches and lunar moths,
there was silence—that peaceful nothing—
was enough, and I sank back into delta mud.

She Wanted Purple Jeans for Christmas

They say purple people really love purple.
And that is so true of my Grandma Carolyn.
If she could, she'd dye all she owns with orchil,
and put food coloring in her chicken-and-dumplings.

Grandma loves her irises, but I hope
one day she'll have violets, lilacs, and bellflower
because she's faithful, loving, gracious, and gold.
Maybe she'll get those with this spring's showers.

I hope she knows that to me, she is mulberry.
Healing, protecting amethyst, and devoted lavender.
A serene periwinkle and strong like my pawpaw's plum trees.
On her irises rests a purple emperor.

The B-Grandkid

When I was just a little kid
my mom's mom thought I was stupid.
My teacher bragged to my parents
about how I'd help other children read a sentence.
Grandma said my teacher lied
and that my mom and dad should have no pride.

Only a few years ago did I learn this was true,
and my grandma died in 2002.
But it felt like learning she'd died all over again.
Except this time, every memory of her, as I'll explain,
was tainted like her lungs when she developed staph,
and then our names were carved into her epitaph.

She wasn't perfect, and she could be mean,
but I believed she loved and believed in me.
Growing up is realizing that can be true, but so can
the fact that she thought her other grandkids were smarter than
me, because at this point, I have a master's degree,
and every day, I teach children to write and read.

None of those things I could do,
if I were stupid, Grandma Linda Lou.
I wish you were alive to see me flourish, almost.
But I wish even more that my mom could boast.
Because you believed she was dumb,
so her kids must also be bums.
Most of all, I wish you could get a glimpse
of how wonderful the daughter you raised is.
And how I, with my published poetry, am an extension of her
and how she is one hundred times the mother you ever were.

To Alyssa:

In these little hours of respite
I've spent in mismatched socks
and a bralette with sleep pants,
chapped lips and wind-bitten cheeks.
I think about you, my best friend,
standing in our apartment in your floral robe
across from the Christmas tree that's still up
in late January.

How we met in elementary school,
little ladybugs on the playground,
but our paths rarely crossed
until high school electives let us fly
in the same loveliness.
We learned it's the name
of a group of ladybugs in science class.
We created mobile games and sang hymns.
We wrote silly, naughty stories
and bonded over Pokémon.

I remember the first time I came to your house,
eating nachos and chicken tenders
because that's what I requested.
Then we watched a goofy vampire movie until
I fell down the stairs to your trailer
spraining my ankle so badly,
I was up at 2 am in pain,
but still thankful I'd gone.

Now you pick up my cat in our living room
meowing back at him and nuzzling his head.
A lightbulb sparks in my brain
at how much I can love someone
so brightly,
like a trusty nightlight,
always glowing and prepared to lead me
out of the dark.

$15 Palm Reading

I sat in the back of an antique store on Bathhouse Row across from a blonde wearing mixed metals on both hands, draped in old wood and patchouli. She had a card table set up with sparkly black fabric over it. Boxes of tarot cards sat on the table and shelves behind her, along with jars of herbs and crystal pendulums. A tropical bird squawked in the other room. A sign said that it bites. At her coaxing, I sat both hands on the table, palms up, so my wrists ached. She pressed and poked on each palm, curled her fingers around my fingers, and spoke of Jupiter and Saturn. She said, "You're a writer, aren't you?" My mouth gaped as I swallowed my tongue. She picked up a quartz the size of my hand, pointed, and held it like a pencil to trace the arid lines on my skin. "But more importantly . . . that generational trauma is not yours to process. *But you can release it.*" Tears filled my eyes as I remembered the fear and control my mother and her sister faced at the hands of their father, how they were defiled and disrespected. "*But* you can release it." I pictured the abuse as a cocoon in my clenched fist, and when I opened it, dozens of butterflies flew away. They were borne from the lines on my palms, tended by the pads on my fingers, and released from the joints connecting them. *But you can release it.*

I took a deep breath and watched them soar.

Written Archaeology

This morning, I got a Facebook invitation
for this year's family reunion on my mother's side.
The one we haven't attended in years.
Disturbing an ancient burial ground that hasn't been cleared.
Just the thought of those people makes
my hands quiver and quake,
Like the Parkinson's and Dementia that ate
my grandpa's brain.

The audacity of that family is startling and gross,
like beetles in the red clay.
They want the past to stay the past,
as if what is buried will stay underground forever.
They never expected me to be born with a shovel
to unearth their unspeakable things.

I'll never let it go, how women weren't safe from ages 0–100
because the older generation was taught
that we were made for them
to do whatever they want
with no consequence.
Meanwhile, the trauma is embedded over four generations.

Or how my mom wasn't good enough,
simply because she was a girl who could not hear.
And her sister was quite literally
the redheaded stepchild,
while her indolent brother
was crowned the heir of the gravel pit.

And how the widow of a beloved uncle
was more welcome than us
when she flirted with the man
who brought my uncle's oxygen
right in front of him as cancer
rendered him speechless
like a statue made from marble.

So have your reunion, your dirt cake, and eat it, too.
But don't expect me to keep my excavation pen to myself.
One day, my books about your sins
will sit upon your shelves.

Familiar

When she comes home, I say hello
with a *mrow mrow.*
Up I go, and she kisses my dark face,
whiskers tickling her cheeks,
Once down, I hop up on my rest
preening and purring.

I follow her to the bedroom,
the floor littered with clothes.
I have to tiptoe on my panther paws.
But sometimes she can't even get out of bed,
and still, she scoops my box every day.

On the bed, I jump
to join her, settling on her chest.
I buzz and slowly blink
to show her I am pleased.
Then I yawn with tuna breath
right into her nose.

Sometimes, she cries so hard
her entire body wracks with shudders.
In these times, I nudge her tears
with the coal of my nose
and meow over the sobs.
She doesn't have to stop.
But I will be there
until she smiles once again.

I Chased You Off Because I Get Attached
Too Quickly

I brought my Oracle cards the night we first met
because they were monster-themed,
and we brainstormed tattoos while you asked me if the cards knew
if you'd be married by the time you turned thirty.
They weren't on your side, but still, I giggled.
And I hoped they were wrong.
Because more than anything,
I wanted matching ring tattoos
with you.

What Little Remains

They duct-taped us together in health class, arm to arm, side to side, and then ripped it off like a Band-Aid from a scraped knee, taking the hairs on my arm with it. It made a shhhh sound. They told me to sit down, and they grabbed another girl. They used the duct tape that linked me to you to stick you to her as if you were roll-on glue. "See?" they said, "it doesn't stick right anymore." The more people you tape together, the less likely they are to bond. It's a dumb metaphor for sex in a Christian sex ed class. Even as a teenager, I knew it was foolish.

Still.

My arm was still tacky with your tape when your footprints disappeared behind the front door. I slept with the strip on my pillow for months. It ripped my hair out and left residue on my cheek. When anyone else tried to glue me to them, it would flit to the floor, unable to adhere. Just like me, the band yearned for you. It will never work again, unstuck to my heart and torn away.

Moths Are Not Butterflies

You came as a surprise,
when you stepped out of your cocoon.
With Luna moth eyes,
shifting gold and emerald,
but dark in the center.

You're not rare but rarely seen,
nocturnal, green, and so high,
I found you in the broadleaf trees,
and mistook you for a green hairstreak,
not knowing our lifespan was so short.

You loved me for less than a fortnight,
it was a ten-day cycle,
where we spread our wings and flew.
But when snow flurries began to fall,
we crashed and burned with the cold front.

Empty Calories

Like a can of Coke, you siphoned me down.
Popped my tab, and when you were through, crushed me
in your hand and stomped me to the wet ground,
littered aluminum for all to see.

Remember when you chose me from the store?
You had stopped for a cold and sweet drink
and your Sprite eyes landed on the fridge door.
Curled your fingers around me, like a ring.

The first time your lips touched me, I swore that
you were my purpose, gave my life meaning.
My carbonation flattening as I sat,
but I faded, my tin hardly gleaming.

They say the life of a can is inert.
I am crumpled red bauxite in the dirt.

From the Dewy Screen Door

I don't rightly know
why the Deep Creek rises
or why the Chuck-will's-widow
only sings at nighttime
when the moon is high
and the stars make up a neon sign.

Spring in the south,
it ain't no count,
full of twisters and flash floods.
Nights spent in a storm cellar,
if you're lucky. Or a bathtub
if you aren't.

Once the drainage ditches flood,
I always find myself thinking
should I drown myself in one of those
or a bottle of rot-gut whiskey?
I don't care which, just as long
as it's siphoned right into my lungs.

Then it's summertime and hotter than blazes
under the blistering delta sun.
One hundred degrees in the shade with
humidity to match, it ain't that fun
even at the local swimming holes.
Just another place to drown.

You know, I'm plumb tired
of trying to convince myself
to stay above the water.
No matter the season, you're in
the back of my brain and the front of my heart.
And me? I'm wading in blood.

G-Note

I'd never met someone who
loved music like I do.
Someone who heard its value,
recognized that nothing was more true.

We bonded over The Story So Far
and how "Take Me As You Please"
gave us all the feels.
I hate that phrase, but that's how you put it.
And the song's title is how I felt about you.
I'd have you however you'd take me.
Parker Cannon sang, "don't write a sad song,"
and we said, "You'll burn out your love" right back.
How I wish it hadn't been so exact.

We made each other countless playlists,
my feelings for you building like a crescendo.
With every song you sent me,
I sang through the sharps and flats
to frame each rhyme around your face.

You told me I looked like Kacey Musgraves,
like her, it made me feel so high.
So how could I have predicted
your "Irish Goodbye"?

You sent your final playlist in November,
the month you and I were both born.
And every time I hear "Take Me As You Please,"

my heart becomes so sore.
I wish you hadn't ruined so many songs for me.
But I wish you loved me more.

I hope you're conducting a joyful symphony
and still making the best playlists.
Even if I can't be part of your orchestra,
maybe I'll put Spotify on shuffle and catch a glimpse.

Deconstruction Surgery

I've written so many poems about you.
I think that this makes ten,
though the others were much more
metaphorical and kind.
This one is to take apart my head,
pull out my brain so I can inspect it
for parasites in the shape of pot plants
and vinyl records and the UFC logo,
all of those things that are permanently yours,
that I'm not allowed to touch anymore.
Like a sculpture in a museum behind glass.
Once my brain is clean of impurities,
I'll give it a good shake: one, two, three.
Then I'll screw it back in like a lightbulb.
If I turn the light on, and I still see your face,
I'll have to pull it back out, and take it to therapy,
discuss cognitive behaviors,
set it up on a light blue chaise
as a woman with a notebook asks it how it feels
to be out of its body,
body without mind.
The brain will tell the shrink that my heart
is who's actually to blame.
The only problem is
it's gone from my body, too.
When you left,
you took it with you.

From the Perspective of the Boy I Wanted
to Marry

It felt like you wanted this to be a country song.
This all started as us sending
each other punk playlists
so why would a country song be ours?
Boy meets girl, girl falls in love, boy also falls in love,
just like Johnny and June.
Riding back roads listening to the radio.
Porch beers on stinging summer
Saturday nights with my buddies and their girlfriends.
Sweet tea and fried chicken on Sundays
after church, but you're not religious.
We listened to secular music on Friday nights,
too hungover for any of those good-old-boy things.

You fell so hard and so fast, it gave me whiplash
I couldn't hold feelings that big in my hands.
They slipped right through onto a hardwood floor,
spilling into the cracks
that now make up your heart.
When the floor was actually concrete
in a city where I made you mine.

But my boots never sat by your door
and I never played guitar for you.
My yard doesn't have a barn
and I have a car, not a truck.
What part of this made you think

we could be Tim and Faith?
Maybe you actually meant
Sid and Nancy.

I never set out to break your heart in halves,
but you have to know it's on you, too.
You expected me to put a ring on your finger
the first month in.
That only happens in country songs
and we all know how those end—
Kacey with no Ruston,
Miranda with no Blake.

Boughs of Melancholy

Your hazel eyes reminded me of lights
on a Christmas tree, wrapping me in wires.
When we'd hang out, I'd check my makeup twice
like Santa and his list by the fire.

Your hair was soft as snow, but colored coal.
That was all you gave me that holiday.
I found the perfect gift for you, straight from the North Pole,
but I never got to send it your way.

The stockings were hung and filled with my love,
but you didn't want the stuffers I hand-picked for you.
I watched you from the chimney above,
tossing the tinsel, I knew we were through.

My angel, who shattered my ornaments
and burned every carol into a lament.

Affectionate Artillery

Your hands were soft guns pointed right at me.
I let them cup my cheeks, barrels on skin.
Your thumbs were triggers, stroking jawlines.
Powder on your fingertips, brushing lips.

Your eyes, gentle knives reflecting green.
I let them pierce right to the hilt.
Your lashes like needles, sharp but fixing.
The forest of your irises, poised to kiss or kill.

Your smile was a time bomb counting down.
I held it in my hands as it glittered.
The seconds ticked by, and it drew me in.
It exploded in my palms, debris in its wake.

You were a heavenly assassin
assigned to capture, draw, and quarter me.
I accepted the torture with bright eyes
because as you dragged me over gravel
I dreamed of your viridescent reverie.

Aubade with a Mockingbird Witness

Chirping interrupts the afterglow.
Yellow light filters in
from the gaps in the black curtains,
illuminating the massive tattoo
on your chest, fluorescent dandelion.
I wake up before you in your marital bed,
ivory sheets, pillows, and a duvet.
I imagine it stained red from last night
when you poured me a glass of merlot,
bed tainted by my hairy body
and leaving a semblance of evidence.

The sound is a mockingbird
at the window, who taunts me
as I try to absorb the ink
that touched you before me,
just like your wife does every other night.
Somehow the bird knows I must leave
before the sun slips back
into place among the clouds,
but your lanky arms hold me like a vise
that I won't make myself escape from.

That bird's song reminds me
of the guitar you taught yourself to play
and the rough calluses you've had on your fingers
since we were fourteen and you became
the best friend I ever had.

How those calluses cup my cheeks,
like a feather's touch, but they also
can grip my hips so hard
they leave bruises in the swirls of your fingertips
so if we dusted my body for prints,
you'd be the prime suspect.

You're still asleep as I wrench myself
out of the heart that doesn't belong to me,
the body I have to share.
You don't have to hear the funeral procession
the mockingbird performs as I pull on my shirt
and close the door.

Blackwork

I want to tattoo my body until there's no skin left,
cover up the scars, raised and angry white,
ink up the heart inside my chest.

I'll start with things you love, like music fests,
smoking weed, horror movies, and UFC fights.
I want to tattoo my body until there's no skin left.

You'll see butterflies and clovers when I'm undressed.
Song lyrics from late nights gone and floral scenes,
inking up the heart inside my chest.

The needles will become one with my arms
to cover the lines, remnants of cardiac arrest.
I want to tattoo my body until there's no skin left.

In the center of my breast, I'll dedicate to you a crest
with shades of purple, red, and green,
inking up the heart inside my chest.

So that maybe in my body you'll become a permanent guest,
run your hands over the healed skin, white.
I'm going to tattoo my body until there's no skin left,
black ink filling up the heart inside my chest.

Drunk Feelings; Sober Thoughts

Maybe it's because I liked you too much and you didn't know.
It would've helped if we'd have talked it over.

Maybe it's because I was just too far away and wanted too much.
I guess I should have taken it slower.

Maybe you weren't ready for all that I wanted.
I was ready to marry a stoner.

Maybe this is all my fault, but maybe it isn't.
Regardless, I don't think I could feel any lower.

Maybe if you'd have just been honest this whole time.
Then maybe I wouldn't have trouble being sober.

11:11 Isn't an Angel Number

I often think about you and how
your birthday is 11/11.
I was born only nine days before. Now,
the cold silence of your absence deafens.

At that time, I'd make the simplest wish:
I'd be yours by divine intervention.
Still, I feared that the shooting star would miss,
if not just from my own intuition.

The eleventh card represents justice,
but I don't think you know what that means since
you left and ghosted all your trust in us.
Still, I stayed present in the moment, tense.

Eleven is the messenger, they say.
Still, I wait for the word as I decay.

Ghosted

I can't call you a ghost because they haunt,
and the way to haunt is to stick around.
You dematerialized in the night.

You disappeared, leaving my heart vexed, taut.
I frantically searched our tower round.
I can't call you a ghost because they haunt.

I grieved without a tombstone, gray and gaunt.
My only company was my black cat.
You dematerialized in the night.

I decomposed, eulogized by mad rats.
In a pillow-thick fog, I thought I'd drowned.
I can't call you a ghost because they haunt.

I thought I'd grow a garden while you watched.
And build a murder of crows and black cats.
You dematerialized in the night.

For now, I will pour a circle of salt.
So my love for you stays sowed in the ground.
I can't call you a ghost because they haunt.
You dematerialized in the night.

Orion's Killer

There's just something about Scorpio boys,
and how I can't escape from their stingers.
With deadly venom, they seek to destroy,
I'm weak in spite of my grasping pincers.

Beautiful, born under an autumn moon,
eyes dark and sleepy, purple underneath,
casting wicked spells disguised as punk tunes.
Tangled in their tales, unable to breathe.

I don't know, maybe it's just narcissism.
I, too, born under that November sign,
but I think it's really masochism,
wanting to be punished by my own kind.

Tortured arachnids dressed like butterflies,
enticing me under cold stone and lies.

On the One That Wasn't the One

When I think of you, I think of
glassy red eyes and perfect white teeth.
I think of Kacey Musgraves and rolling papers,
the Story so Far and Scorpio season.
When I think of you, I think of
smiles and giddy horror nights.
I think of long drives and Spotify playlists.
Jameson and weed and introverted silence.

When I think of you, I think of
all the times you let me down.
I think of the birthday presents you never gave me.
All the messages you ignored and my heart bleeding on the floor.
When I think of you, I think of
growth and stitching myself back together.
I wonder if you even think of me.

That Time I Stole the Sky

Once I dreamt of yanking stars from the black sky,
lining my pockets until they were so full
they jangled and jingled when I walked.
But then I woke to empty pockets and a blazing sun
so hot it stung my skin through a flapping curtain.
That heat reminded me of one summer day
when I picked a bouquet of red roses for you,
only for you to tell me you preferred white lilies.
I won't touch a lily, as they're fatal to cats
and my cat is like a star to me, pulled right from a black sky.

Once I dreamt of yanking the moon from the black sky,
hanging it in my room in lieu of a nightlight.
But then I woke to angry gray clouds,
rain pitter-pattering on my bedroom window.
That rain reminded me of buying you a hot chocolate
only for you to say a vanilla latte was your favorite drink.
I love a vanilla latte, too,
but only on ice, and that's inappropriate
for a cold, rainy day,
water pulled right from a black sky.

Once I dreamt of yanking down the black sky,
pulling it into the sea until the heavens were bright blue.
But then I woke to an early sunset,
pushing and pulling the ether down,
an orange, rosy, and azure creamsicle
shadowing the glass casement.

That creamsicle reminded me of baking an apple pie
just for you
to accept a cherry souffle from someone else
on a late-night cruise
underneath the black sky.

About the Author

An Arkansas delta native, Kalina Smith is mostly a poet, though she also writes fiction and creative nonfiction. She teaches high school English and creative writing, where she spends her days nurturing young storytellers and navigating the emotional labor of the classroom. Outside of teaching, she enjoys spending time with her black cat, Gus, and her friends and family, trying to be a novice lepidopterist, attending way too many pop punk shows, and scaring herself with true crime and horror.

Her work appears in *Nebo, The Ignatian, FLARE: The Flagler Review, ONE ART BY A Journal of Poetry, RedRoseThorns,* and many others, with work forthcoming in *Porcupine, Superfan, Micromance,* and more. She served as poetry editor for *Shadowplay* during the Spring of 2025.

Instagram:
@kalinasmithpoetry

Website:
kalinasmith.com